AF207606

LITTLE WOMEN

by
Louisa May Alcott

Student Packet

Written by
Stacie Champlin Dreibrodt

Contains masters for:

2	Pre-reading Activities
10	Vocabulary Activities
4	Literary Analysis Activities
5	Character Analysis Activities
4	Writing Activities
2	Comprehension Quizzes
1	Final Exam

Plus   Detailed Answer Key

Note

The Apple Classics Paperback, a division of Scholastic Inc., abridged version was used to prepare this guide. The page references may differ in the hardcover or other paperback editions.

To order, contact your local school supply store, or—

Novel Units, Inc.
P.O. Box 97
Bulverde, TX 78163-0097

Web site: www.educyberstor.com

Directions: Rate the following statements before you read the novel. Compare and discuss your ratings with a partner. After you have completed the novel, discuss the ratings again in light of the story.

1 ———— 2 ———— 3 ———— 4 ———— 5 ———— 6
strongly agree   strongly disagree

	Before	**After**
1. Families should always support each other.	_____	_____
2. It is hard to be happy with your life when you do not have much money.	_____	_____
3. It is difficult to maintain a relationship with someone when he/she lives far away.	_____	_____
4. You should always look out for yourself.	_____	_____
5. If you do not have much, you need not worry about trying to help others.	_____	_____
6. You cannot help the way you feel about someone.	_____	_____
7. Doing something nice for someone else makes you feel good about yourself.	_____	_____
8. Children are too young to handle tough situations.	_____	_____
9. Being happy with your life is a choice everyone must make.	_____	_____
10. If possible, one should try to marry someone with money.	_____	_____
11. Bad things only happen to bad people.	_____	_____
12. Adults always know what is best for children.	_____	_____
13. Siblings should always look out for each other.	_____	_____
14. There is never a time when you should accept charity from others.	_____	_____
15. You cannot trust anyone other than yourself and your family.	_____	_____
16. Raising a family takes more than one person doing all of the work.	_____	_____

Directions: Think about each idea listed below. Free write about each one. Try to write about each word for at least five minutes. Use extra paper if needed. Be prepared to discuss your thoughts with classmates.

1. loyalty

2. family

3. promise

4. freedom

5. maturity

6. responsibility

7. pride

8. dignity

Name_____

Chapters 1-4—pages 1-26
1. Why won't Christmas be the same?
2. Where is Father?
3. After talking longer, what do the girls decide to do with their money?
4. What did Father go off to war as?
5. What are the girls to find under their pillows Christmas morning?
6. Where is Mother on Christmas morning?
7. What do the girls do with their breakfast?
8. How does Mrs. Hummel refer to the girls?
9. What language do the Hummels speak?
10. What do the girls do to entertain themselves?
11. Who sent them dessert and flowers? Why?
12. What does Beth fear?
13. What are Jo and Meg invited to attend?
14. Why does Jo have to stand with her back against the wall?
15. Who does Jo run into as she is trying to escape a dance partner?
16. What happens to Meg as she dances?
17. Why do the girls always turn and look back toward the house?
18. What did Aunt March offer to do with one of the girls?
19. Why didn't the March family accept Aunt's offer?
20. What does Jo utilize while at Aunt March's?
21. The older gentleman who is unable to go to war gave what to his country instead?

Chapters 5-8—pages 26-52
1. What does Jo intend to do about young Laurence?
2. What does Jo take with her on her visit?
3. What does Jo discover that the two have in common?
4. Why does Jo tell Laurie he should be the happiest boy in the world?
5. What does Mr. Laurence tell Jo about her grandfather?
6. What does Mr. Laurence notice about his grandson in Jo's presence?
7. What happened to Laurie's parents?
8. What does Mr. Laurence offer to allow the girls to use?
9. What do the Laurences do to promote Beth's playing?
10. What does Beth do for Mr. Laurence?
11. What does Mr. Laurence do upon receipt of the slippers?
12. Who does Mr. Laurence tell Beth she reminds him of?
13. What does Beth do to thank him?
14. What does Amy need money for?
15. What does Jenny do to get Amy in trouble?

---

16. What does Amy have to do with the limes?
17. What does Amy do about school?
18. Where are Jo and Meg going?
19. What does Jo wonder about during the show?
20. What does Jo discover is missing?
21. What does Amy do to get back at Jo?
22. Where does Jo intend to go with Laurie?
23. What does Amy not hear about the ice?
24. What does Mother tell Jo about her temper?

Chapters 9-12—pages 52-77

1. Where is Meg going?
2. What does Meg receive from Laurie?
3. What does Meg overhear the girls talking about?
4. What does Laurie tell Meg about how he feels about her new look?
5. What does Meg tell Laurie when he says she shouldn't drink much champagne?
6. How does Mother respond to the knowledge of gossip?
7. What club do the girls pretend to be in?
8. Who do they allow to join the group?
9. What does Laurie set up for the girls?
10. What does Mother think the girls will discover about all play and no work?
11. What happens to Pip, the canary? Why?
12. What does Jo put on the berries?
13. What does Jo receive from her mother in the P.O. box?
14. What does Laurie invite the girls to do?
15. What does Amy do while she sleeps?
16. Who does Laurie think is the prettiest?
17. Who does he like the most?
18. What will Laurie do next year?

Chapters 13-16—pages 78-104

1. Where does Jo assume Laurie was?
2. What does she tell him when he says he was not in the saloon?
3. What is Jo doing in town?
4. What secret does Laurie tell Jo?
5. Why does Jo act so silly for the next two weeks?
6. What information does Mrs. March receive in a telegram?
7. What is Mother expecting to do for Father?

8. What does Aunt March write to Mother?
9. What does Jo go out and do?
10. Why is Jo crying?
11. What is the girls' motto?
12. What does Beth do at the window?
13. What news do they have on Father?
14. Where does Jo find Beth?
15. What does Beth tell Jo about the Hummels' baby?
16. How does the doctor treat Mrs. Hummel? Why?
17. Why must Amy go to Aunt March's house?
18. What does Laurie do for the girls that would make Jo happy?
19. What happens with Beth?
20. What does Amy have to do while at Aunt March's house?
21. What does Esther allow Amy to do?
22. What is Esther going to set up for Amy?
23. What else does Esther help Amy do?

Chapters 17-20—pages 104-125
1. How does Mother react to the knowledge of Amy's sanctuary?
2. Who is the picture of in the sanctuary?
3. What does Aunt March give Amy?
4. How does Amy convince Mother to allow her to wear the ring?
5. What does Jo tell Mother about Meg?
6. Why won't Mr. Brooke make Meg aware of this?
7. What does Mother inform Jo about John?
8. How old must Meg be before she marries?
9. Why is Jo acting strange around Meg?
10. Why doesn't Jo wish to spend the day with Laurie?
11. Who does Meg think wrote the letter?
12. What does the note say?
13. What does Meg do with the note?
14. What does Meg write in response?
15. How does John respond to Meg's note?
16. Who does Jo think wrote both letters?
17. What knowledge does Laurie tell Meg that comforts her?
18. What present does Laurie give the Marches for Christmas?
19. What does Father say about Meg's hand?
20. What happened to Jo, according to Father?
21. What about Beth?

22. What does Father say about Amy?
23. What has happened to Meg concerning John?
24. What does John ask of Meg in return for his taking care of her father?
25. What happens to the speech Meg had prepared?
26. What does Meg finally tell John?
27. What does Aunt March tell Meg will happen if she chooses to marry John?
28. What does Meg tell Aunt March?
29. According to Aunt March, why does John like Meg?
30. What does Meg tell John when he returns?
31. What does Jo find upon entering the parlor?
32. John refers to Jo in what way?
33. What does John tell the Marches?

Chapters 21-25—pages 126-153

1. How much time has now passed?
2. What is Mr. March doing?
3. What had John done?
4. After returning home, what did John do?
5. What are each of the girls doing now?
6. What is Laurie doing?
7. What does Aunt March take back?
8. What does Aunt March do for Meg when she and John get married?
9. What does Laurie bring Meg?
10. What does Laurie want from his grandfather?
11. What does Laurie tell Jo about marriage?
12. How does Jo reply?
13. What does Meg want instead of a fashionable wedding?
14. Why is Aunt March so upset?
15. Who tries to dance with Aunt March?
16. What does Aunt March do?
17. According to Amy, what are desirable qualities?
18. What is Amy planning at the end of her drawing class?
19. What happens on the day of Amy's party?
20. Why does Amy have to go into town?
21. What good fortune does Jo encounter?
22. What does Meg set out to do?
23. What agreement do John and Meg make about their private affairs and problems?
24. What does John choose to do on "jelly day"?
25. What do John and the guest do?

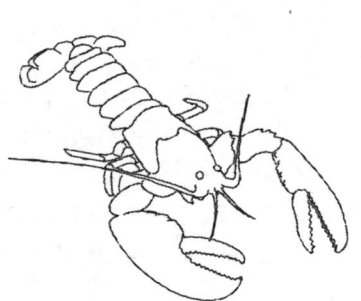

26. What does John tell Lotty to do with the jelly and the pots?
27. What does Laurie discover at Meg's?
28. Who are the babies named after?

Chapters 26-28—pages 153-177
1. What type of calls are the girls discussing?
2. How does Jo behave at the first house?
3. What does Jo do at the Lambs' house?
4. How does Jo insult Miss Lamb?
5. What is Jo's philosophy about pretending to have things?
6. How does Jo behave at the third house?
7. Why does Amy get angry with Jo about the boys she chooses to be nice to?
8. What is the problem between Amy and May?
9. What does Mrs. Chester ask Amy to do at the fair?
10. What do Jo and Laurie plan to bring to the fair?
11. What news does Mrs. March receive from Aunt Carrol?
12. What does Jo now wish she hadn't said in front of the aunts?
13. What does Amy hope to find out in Rome?
14. What are we told at the end of chapter 27?
15. What is Mother worried about?
16. What does Jo think is wrong with Beth?
17. How did Laurie's behavior change while he was away?
18. What does Jo tell Laurie about flirting?
19. What advice does Jo give Laurie?
20. What does Jo want to do in the winter?

Chapters 29-31—pages 177-198
1. Who has Jo become interested in learning more about?
2. What does Jo decide to do for Professor Bhaer?
3. What does the professor offer to do for Jo in return?
4. What does the professor give Jo?
5. What does Jo decide to do with her writings?
6. Why does the editor remove some of the moral passages?
7. What is Jo planning to do with the money she earns?
8. What does Jo do to find ideas for stories?
9. What kind of information is Jo looking for?
10. According to Jo, why is Professor Bhaer so popular?
11. What does Jo decide is a better possession than money, rank, intellect, or beauty?

12. How does Jo feel about the stories she publishes in *The Weekly Volcano*?
13. What does Jo do with her stories?
14. What does Jo hope to do with the professor's friendship?
15. What does Jo expect Laurie to say on the walk toward home?
16. Why did Laurie change?
17. What does Jo tell Laurie?
18. How is Laurie taking the news?
19. What does Jo tell Mr. Laurence?
20. What do Laurie and Mr. Laurence decide to do together?

Chapters 32-36—pages 198-224

1. How does Beth respond to the idea of the mountain trip?
2. Is it Laurie that Beth is upset about?
3. What is Beth expecting to happen to her?
4. What does Beth want Jo to do for her?
5. Who does Laurie meet up with while abroad?
6. How does Amy describe Laurie?
7. What does Amy plan to do with Laurie?
8. What does Amy notice about Laurie after they finish dancing?
9. What does Laurie notice about Amy?
10. What does Amy ask Laurie about his grandfather?
11. How is Amy different from Laurie when it comes to work?
12. What does Amy notice about Laurie's expression at the mention of Jo?
13. What does Laurie ask Amy about Fred?
14. What is the reason Amy claims she despises Laurie?
15. What does Laurie say when Amy says she wishes Jo were there?
16. What reason does Amy give for speaking to Laurie in such a rude manner?
17. What does Laurie tell Amy in his note?
18. What has been done for Beth?
19. What does Beth say about the needle?
20. Why doesn't Jo ever leave Beth's side?
21. What happens to Beth?
22. How does Laurie intend to earn Jo's respect and admiration?
23. When Laurie comes home, how does Jo respond?
24. How does Amy respond to Fred's proposal?
25. How does Amy learn of Beth's death?
26. Why doesn't Amy return home?
27. What do Amy and Laurie discover when he comes to comfort her?

Chapters 37-41—pages 224-248

1. How does Jo feel now that Beth is gone?
2. What does Mother encourage Jo to do?
3. What news comes concerning Amy and Laurie?
4. How is the news taken?
5. How old is Jo going to be on her birthday?
6. What does Laurie tell Jo about Amy?
7. Why did they get married in Paris?
8. What does Laurie tell Jo about his feelings for her?
9. Who appears at the door of the March home?
10. What does Laurie say he plans to do?
11. What does Amy plan to do?
12. What does Laurie think Professor Bhaer has come for?
13. What are Laurie's concerns?
14. How does Amy respond?
15. How has Jo changed?
16. Why is Jo afraid to admit she is in love?
17. Where does Jo go first when she heads into town?
18. Who does Jo discover during the rain?
19. What does he offer to do for Jo?
20. What does the professor say about how long he will be staying?
21. How does he sound when he shares this news?
22. What opportunity does the professor have?
23. Where is the place he will be teaching?
24. What does the professor ask Jo to help him do in town?
25. How does Jo respond when the professor asks about her tears?
26. What does the professor ask Jo about their relationship?
27. What brought Professor Bhaer to Jo?
28. What does the professor ask Jo if she can do?
29. What good fortune happens to Jo?
30. What does Jo intend to do with the house?
31. What do they celebrate each year at the Bhaers' house?
32. How old is Mrs. March?
33. What does Amy name her daughter?
34. How does Jo describe the life she thought she once wanted?
35. How do all of the women end up?
36. Who do the girls think is responsible for their happy lives?

grumbled (1)	contentedly (1)	altered (1)	sacrifices (1)
statirical (2)	dignity (2)	recesses (3)	chrysanthemums (3)
atmosphere (3)	timid (3)	hearth (4)	dramatic (4)
machinery (5)	chaplain (5)	affection (6)	celestial (6)
hobgoblins (7)	renouncing (7)	slough (7)	despond (7)
hastily (8)	abashed (8)	heroically (9)	buckwheats (9)
procession (9)	gruel (10)	enacted (10)	escort (10)
tumultuous (11)	capital (11)	garret (12)	poplins (13)
exertions (13)	snood (14)	jovial (15)	dwindled (15)
forlornly (15)	demeanor (16)	blunderbus (19)	arnica (20)
dismally (20)	fretting (21)	horrid (21)	implored (21)
momentary (21)	blighted (22)	cultivate (22)	discontented (22)
irascible (23)	affliction (23)	aristocratic (24)	Grecian (24)
console (24)	quenched (24)	dismal (24)	carnelian (25)
recitation (25)	soberly (26)		

Directions: Think about the characters listed below. Write each vocabulary word under the character you associate with that word. (There may be more than one way to sort the words.) Be prepared to support your decisions about where the words belong.

Meg	Jo	Beth	Amy	Mrs. March

On another sheet of paper, write a paragraph about one of the characters listed in the chart. The paragraph should include at least half of the vocabulary words you listed under that character's name.

betokening (27)	wistfully (27)	blancmange (28)	beckoned (29)
solitary (30)	reveled (30)	immensely (30)	quaint (31)
obliged (31)	dismay (31)	abruptly (32)	courtesy (33)
vivacity (33)	conservatory (33)	amiss (34)	inquiring (35)
disposition (35)	plague (35)	enticements (36)	anecdotes (36)
blithely (38)	crotchety (39)	deliberately (40)	cordially (41)
centaur (41)	pardonable (42)	consigned (42)	pretense (43)
contraband (43)	obediently (43)	composure (43)	conscience (43)
portentous (43)	infringed (43)	ignominious (44)	anteroom (44)
indignation (44)	benignant (44)	corporal (45)	conceited (45)
mischievous (45)	bridled (46)	coaxingly (46)	pacify (48)
abominable (49)	penitent (51)		

Directions: Write each vocabulary word on a slip of paper (one word per piece). Make a spinner like the one below and play the following game with a classmate. (*It is good to have a dictionary and thesaurus handy.*) Place papers in a small container. The first player draws a word then spins the spinner and follows the direction where the pointer lands. For example, if the player draws "trolley" and lands on "define," he/she must define the word. If the player's partner accepts the answer as correct, the first player scores one point, and play passes to the second player. If the player's partner challenges the answer, the first player uses a dictionary or thesaurus to prove the answer is correct. If the player can prove the answer is correct, he/she earns two points. If the player cannot prove the answer is correct, the opposing player earns two points. Play continues until all words have been used. The player with the most points wins.

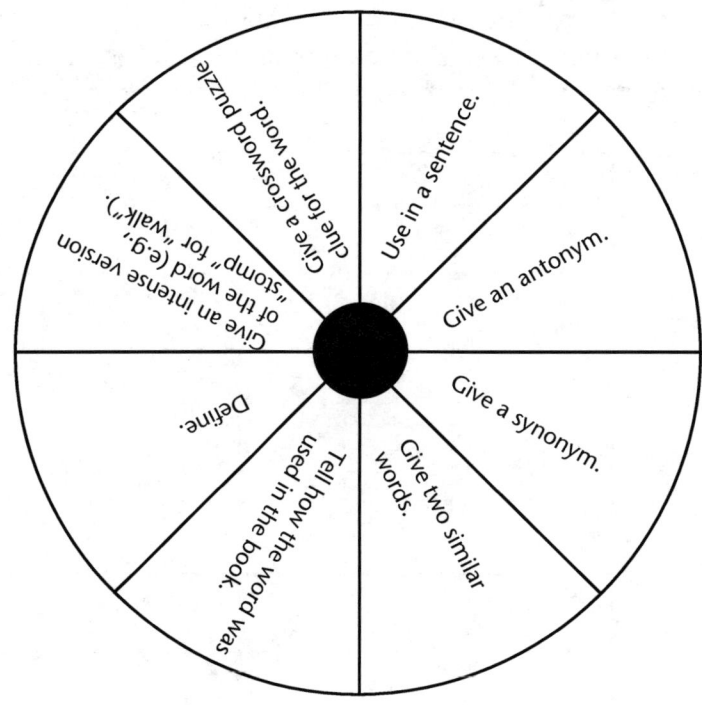

fortnight (52)	relics (52)	daunted (53)	splendor (53)
frolicked (53)	talisman (54)	evidently (54)	agitated (55)
coralline (56)	enthusiastic (56)	abashed (57)	particle (57)
petulantly (57)	languid (58)	indignantly (59)	triumphantly (61)
complacently (63)	bower (63)	inquisitive (63)	muslin (63)
peculiar (64)	variable (64)	bewildered (64)	saleratus (64)
chagrin (64)	culinary (65)	prudently (65)	spectacle (65)
apparition (66)	spinster (66)	assuaged (68)	inaudibly (68)
amiable (69)	postmistress (69)	nosegay (69)	sincerity (70)
resolution (70)	propriety (71)	rations (71)	remonstrated (72)
prospect (72)	averison (72)	wickets (72)	skirmishes (73)
exultation (73)	pretense (74)	nettles (74)	preside (74)
array (74)	venerable (75)	adjourned (75)	Rigmarole (75)
disdainful (76)	intonation (76)	impromptu (77)	amicable (77)

Directions: Choose ten vocabulary words from the list above and write each one in the middle column of the chart below. Write an antonym for each word in the left-hand column. Write a synonym for each word in the right-hand column.

Antonym	Vocabulary Word	Synonym

wistful (78)	earnest (78)	receptacle (78)	omnibus (78)
alighting (78)	manoeuver (78)	rumpled (81)	cherub (81)
woebegone (81)	scandalized (82)	condescension (82)	pathetic (82)
countenance (82)	solemnity (82)	pensively (83)	invalid (85)
indifferent (87)	spire (87)	diverted (87)	christened (89)
omen (89)	accustomed (90)	correspondence (90)	virtue (90)
pendulum (90)	avisiting (90)	shorn (90)	camphor (90)
belladonna (90)	gallivanting (92)	bidden (93)	relapse (93)
cockles (95)	hysterically (95)	lament (96)	docile (97)
amiable (97)	reposed (99)	solace (100)	affianced (100)
promenaded (101)	brocade (101)	petticoat (101)	bequeethe (102)
marshay (102)	affliction (102)	codicils (103)	

Directions: Pick ten words from the above list and create your own word webs.

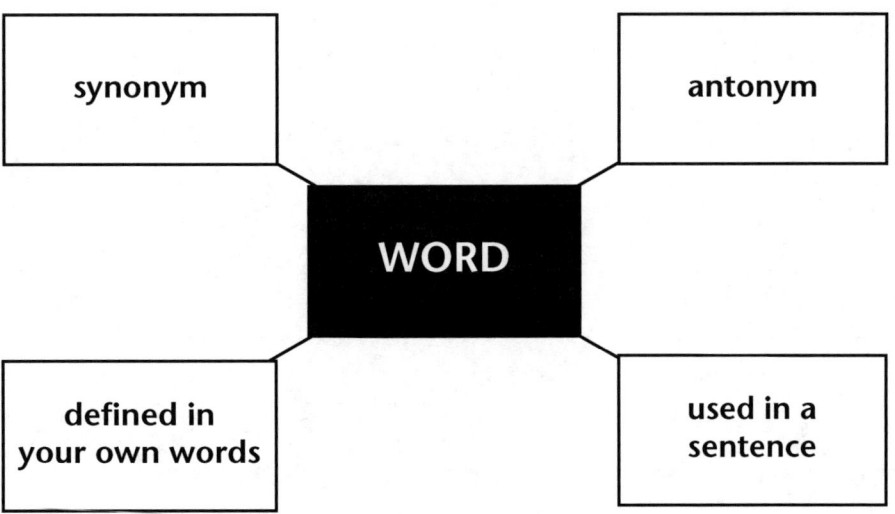

fatigue (104)	vex (105)	consent (107)	conscientious (107)
contraries (108)	patronizing (108)	dignified (108)	bade (108)
corrigible (108)	coax (108)	dint (108)	perseverance (108)
indignant (108)	retaliation (108)	reproachfully (109)	roguish (110)
culprit (111)	sentinel (111)	malicious (112)	suppressed (114)
treacherously (114)	incoherently (114)	feeble (114)	subsided (114)
glowered (115)	accompaniment (117)	quaint (117)	pettishly (118)
trifle (118)	sidle (119)	capricious (120)	evident (121)
peony (121)	peremptorily (121)	inclination (121)	perversity (121)
resolute (121)	indignantly (122)	inconsistent (122)	folly (123)
dudgeon (123)	serenely (123)	abject (124)	eloquence (124)
dismal (124)			

Directions: Write a summary for Part One of *Little Women*. Use at least fifteen of the above vocabulary words in the summary.

_____

_____

_____

_____

_____

_____

_____

_____

_____

_____

_____

_____

_____

_____

parish (126)	resigned (126)	diligently (126)	frolicked (127)
perilously (127)	atonement (127)	exploits (127)	profusion (127)
regiments (127)	quandary (128)	wrath (128)	unassuming (130)
provocation (130)	surveying (131)	offending (131)	ceremonious (132)
moire (132)	momentary (132)	availed (133)	pervaded (134)
dutiful (134)	ambitious (135)	tribulation (135)	inspiration (135)
audacity (135)	pastoral (135)	swarthy (135)	buoy (136)
subsided (136)	picturesque (136)	obstinacy (137)	indignantly (138)
trifling (138)	exasperating (138)	perishable (139)	procured (140)
beguiled (140)	tedium (140)	refractory (140)	vulgar (140)
reminiscences (140)	diverted (140)	rivulets (141)	irksome (141)
cordial (141)	vestige (141)	surfeit (142)	allude (142)
vortex (143)	despondent (143)	labyrinth (143)	elopment (144)
jubilee (144)	reverential (145)	bewilderment (145)	sumptuously (146)
coquettish (146)	unpardonable (147)	irrepressible (147)	pungent (147)
consternation (148)	pinafore (148)	gesture (148)	reproach (148)
conducive (149)	repose (149)	defiance (149)	hospitably (150)
languished (150)	piques (151)	initiated (152)	

Directions: Divide into groups. Within the group, assign each person five vocabulary words from the list above. Use the graphic organizer below to create in-depth webs for each word.

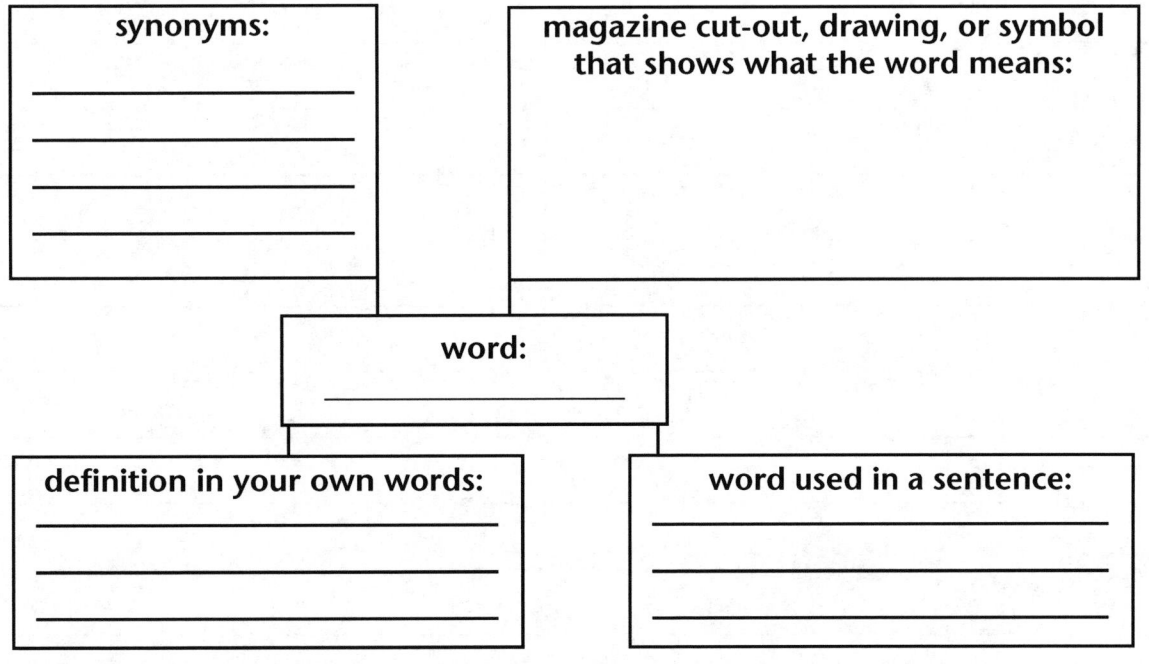

shirking (154)	compelled (154)	organdy (154)	ravishing (154)
deportment (155)	covert (155)	effusion (156)	volubly (156)
brusque (156)	pining (157)	droll (157)	nobility (158)
bespattered (158)	dilapidated (158)	acquaintance (158)	civilly (158)
reprovingly (158)	confiding (150)	consequences (161)	duly (161)
culprits (161)	expediency (162)	consciencestricken (162)	illuminations (162)
disconsolately (162)	adhered (163)	conspirators (165)	gallantly (165)
exonerate (166)	conciliatory (166)	aspirant (168)	philosophic (168)
ferment (168)	stoutly (168)	evaded (169)	distressed (169)
dejectedly (170)	apprehensively (170)	reverie (170)	ardent (170)
alternations (171)	resignation (171)	barricade (171)	stern (171)
aversion (172)	pummelled (172)	extravagances (172)	eligible (173)
admonitory (173)	acquiesced (173)	humility (173)	pondering (174)
infinite (176)	forbearance (176)	tragical (176)	leisure (177)

Directions: Write a poem based on what you have read in the novel. Use at least ten vocabulary words from the list above.

_____

_____

_____

_____

_____

_____

_____

_____

_____

_____

_____

_____

_____

_____

Name_____

prim (179)   seminary (180)   conferred (183)   charity (183)
emboldened (185)   genial (186)   symposium (186)   ethereal (187)
ambling (187)   coveted (188)   revolutions (190)   commencement (190)
motive (191)   exulted (191)   allayed (192)   stalwart (192)
impetuosity (192)   stile (193)   remorsefully (193)   implored (195)
instinct (196)

Directions: Pick eight words from the list above that you want to become more familiar with. List the word in the left-hand column. Write the definition in the middle column. Draw a picture that will help you remember the word in the right-hand column.

Word	Definition	Picture

vague (199)	capitally (202)	prinked (203)	chasséed (204)
tranquilly (204)	decorously (205)	cotillion (205)	gallopaded (205)
alacrity (205)	quizzical (205)	demurely (205)	dwadling (206)
immaculate (207)	perpetual (207)	villa (207)	balustrade (207)
terrace (207)	depravity (208)	indolence (208)	listless (208)
effigy (209)	prudence (210)	dignified (210)	gridiron (211)
significance (212)	diplomatically (212)	adieux (215)	exult (215)
capricious (216)	applicable (216)	fervent (217)	mar (217)
benediction (218)	placid (218)	compose (218)	requiem (218)
plaintive (218)	beset (218)	desultory (219)	pensive (220)
quay (221)	mademoiselle (221)	chateau (221)	subterranean (221)
tempestuous (223)	utterance (223)		

Directions: Create a crossword puzzle using at least twenty of the vocabulary words listed above. You may use a clue, the definition, or the actual sentence from the book. You might want to use a dictionary to help you. Be sure to work your own puzzle to make sure it is correct.

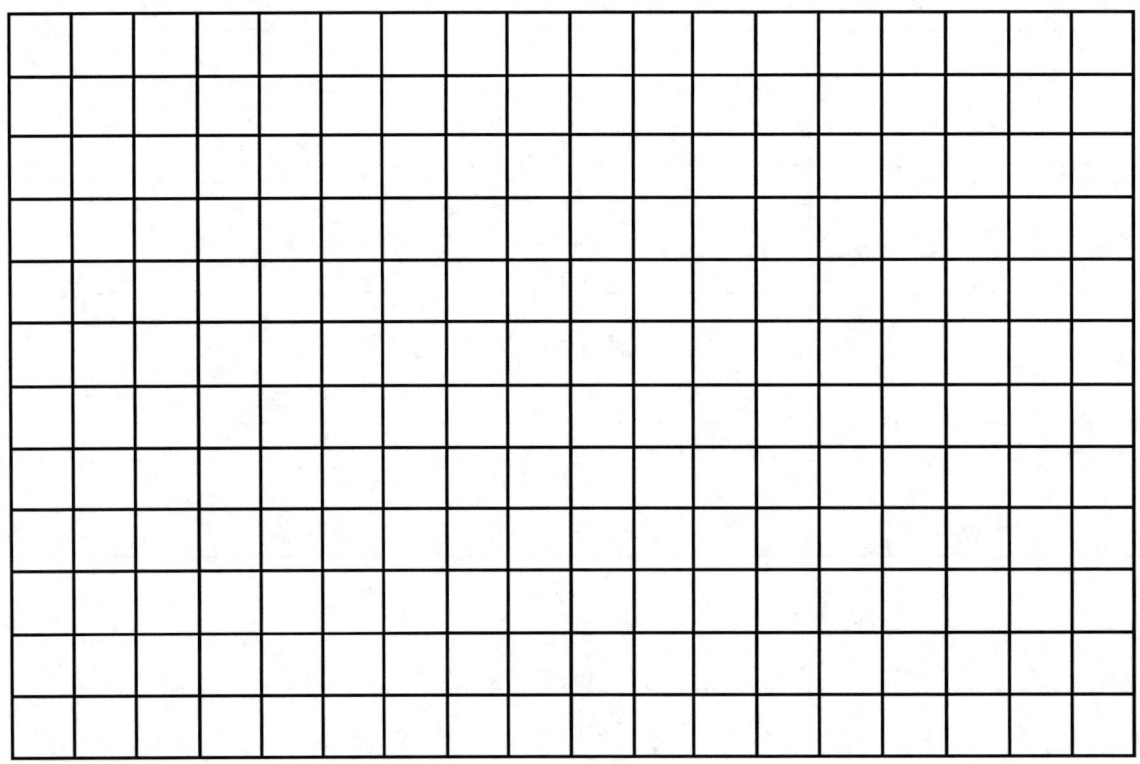

abnegation (224)   toiled (225)   falter (225)   submissive (225)
astonished (226)   pathos (227)   mirth (229)   hale (231)
cordial (232)   query (233)   whiffle (235)   impertinence (235)
sodden (237)   decorous (238)   sternly (238)   coat-of-arms (238)
silesia (238)   loitering (238)   annihilation (239)   distorting (240)
lunatics (242)   voluminous (243)   menagerie (244)   affectionate (244)
confiding (244)   lofty (246)   relinquish (247)   sowing (248)
reaping (248)   tares (248)

Directions: Write a summary for Part Two of *Little Women*. Use at least fifteen of the vocabulary words listed above in your summary.

_____

_____

_____

_____

_____

_____

_____

_____

_____

_____

_____

_____

_____

_____

_____

_____

Main Idea and Supporting Details

Directions: Use the following graph to determine the main idea and supporting details of the novel. Write your explanation of the main idea in the top rectangular box. In the ovals, write the supporting details that go along with the main idea. Be prepared to support your answer. Make sure your supporting details help you accomplish that.

Sequencing

Directions: Use the sequencing circle to put the main events of the novel in the correct order. Once that is completed, write a brief paragraph summarizing the story. Use the transition words given to help you.

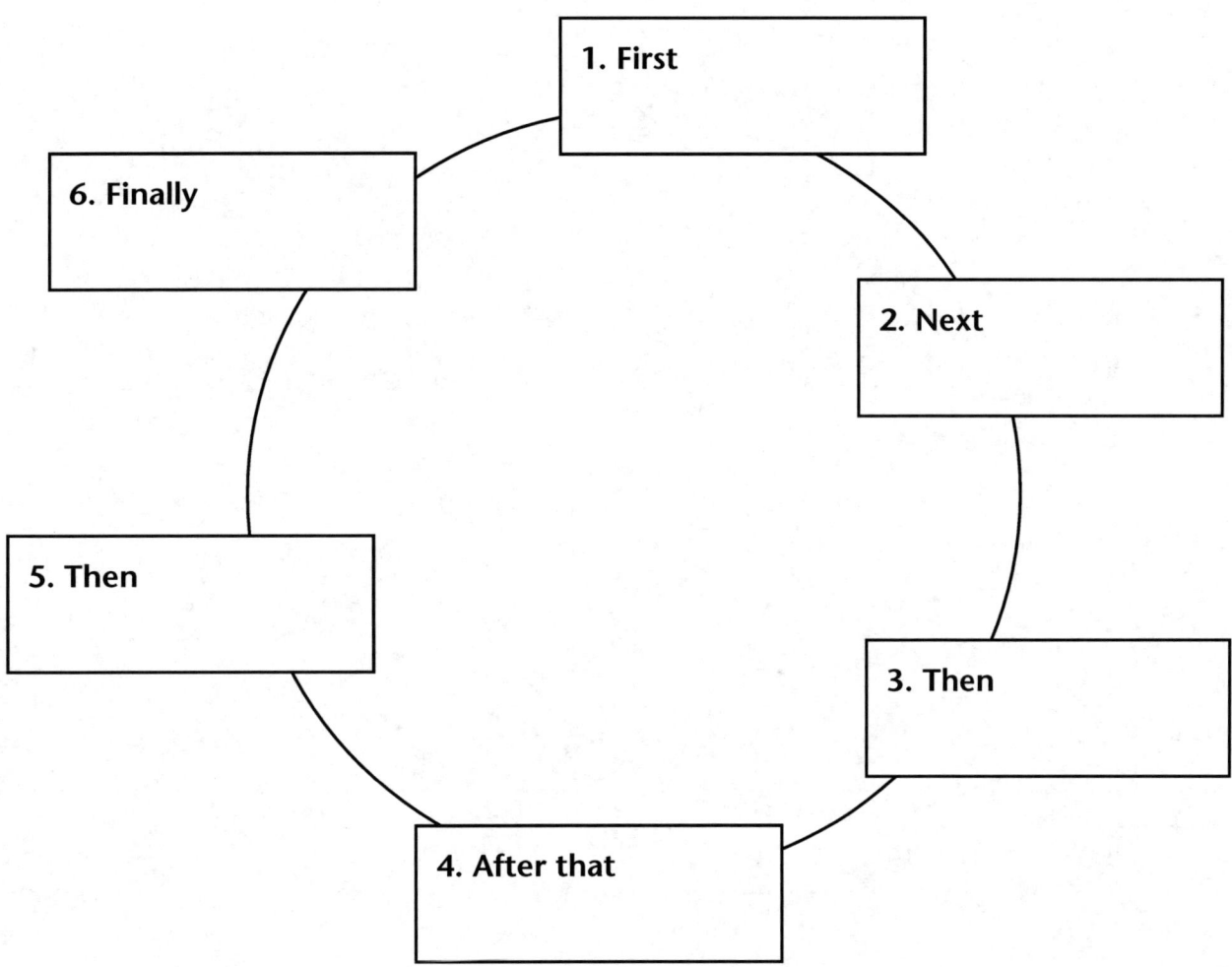

Compare/Contrast

Directions: Use the following graphic organizer to compare/contrast Jo (or one of the other characters) and her life to you and your life. Once you have completed the chart, use it as an aid to write a brief essay.

Jo's Life   **Your Life**

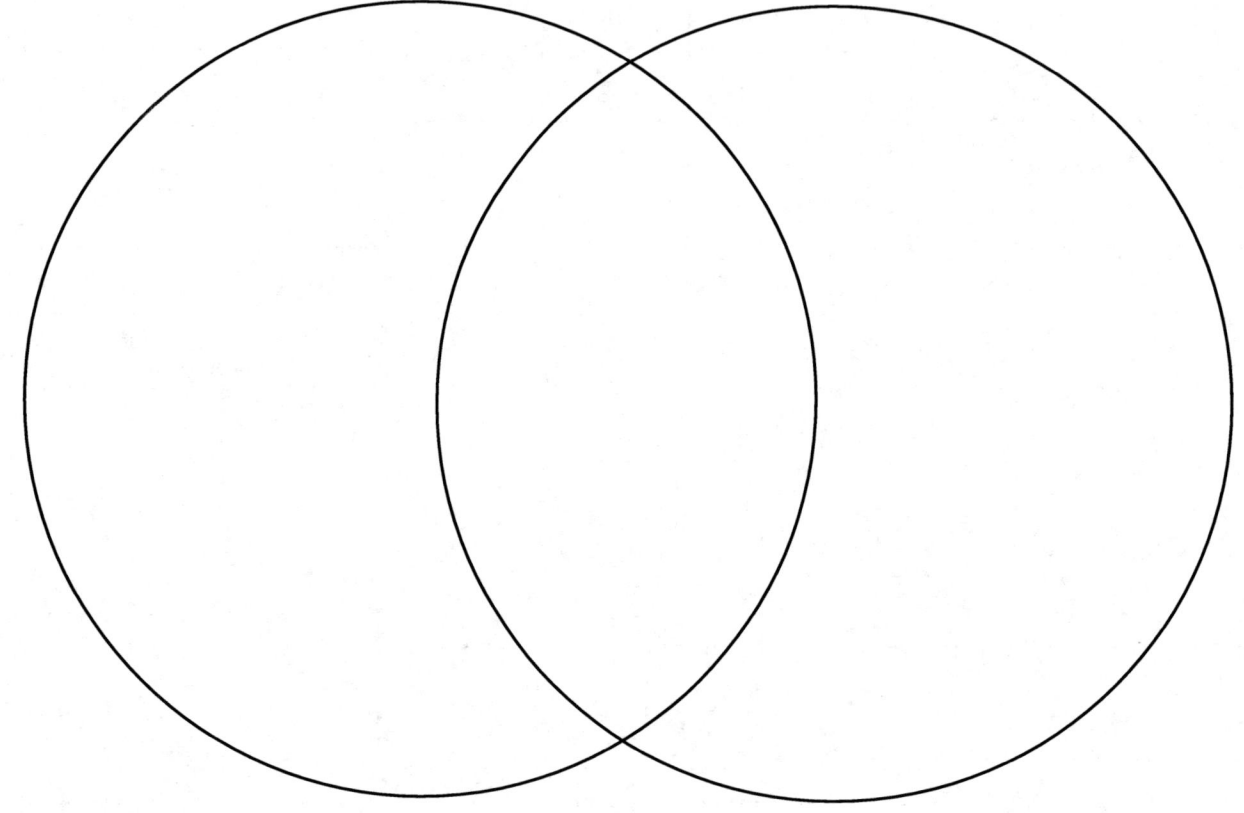

The March Family Motto

Directions: The March family motto is "hope and keep busy." There are many ways that can be interpreted and applied to one's life. Using that philosophy and any others you were able to get from the novel, pretend you are a member of the March family. Create a collection of philosophies and suggestions for living that the Marches would enjoy.

_____

_____

_____

_____

_____

_____

_____

_____

_____

_____

_____

_____

_____

_____

_____

_____

_____

Name_____

Jo's Life

Directions: Throughout the story, Jo goes through numerous changes. What do you think is the main change that occurs in Jo's life? Try to determine the reason behind this change. Can you narrow it down to one event, or are there numerous events that led to the change? Be sure to support your answers and ideas with evidence from the text.

_____

_____

_____

_____

_____

_____

_____

_____

_____

_____

_____

_____

_____

_____

_____

_____

_____

_____

_____

_____

Little Women II

Directions: We live in a world full of sequels. Write your own sequel to *Little Women*. What do you think each one of the characters will be doing in five or ten years? Be sure to include all of the characters.

_____

_____

_____

_____

_____

_____

_____

_____

_____

_____

_____

_____

_____

_____

_____

_____

Sacrifices

Directions: The March family had to go without many things we enjoy today. What three things would you not be able to give up if you were put in their situation? Why? Be sure to think through your answers and support them with good reasons.

_____

_____

_____

_____

_____

_____

_____

_____

_____

_____

_____

_____

_____

_____

_____

Conflict

The conflict of a story is the struggle between two people or two forces. There are three main types of conflict: person against person (PP), person against nature or society (PN), and person against himself/herself (PS).

Directions: The characters in *Little Women* experience many conflicts during the story. In the chart below, list the names of three major characters from the story. In the left column, list two conflicts each character experiences and indicate which conflict is involved (PP, PN, PS). In the right column, explain how each conflict is resolved in the story.

Character:

Conflict	Resolution

Character:

Conflict	Resolution

Character:

Conflict	Resolution

Understanding Values

Directions: Values represent people's beliefs about what is important, good or worthwhile. For example, most families consider spending time together as very important—it is something they value. Think about the following characters from *Little Women*: Meg, Jo, Beth, Amy, Laurie, Mrs. March. What do they value? What beliefs do they have about what is important, good or worthwhile? On the chart below, list each character's three most important values, from most important to least. Be prepared to share your lists during a class discussion. After you have finished the chart and participated in the class discussion, think about which character seems to have values most like your own. Write a paragraph that explains why you chose this character.

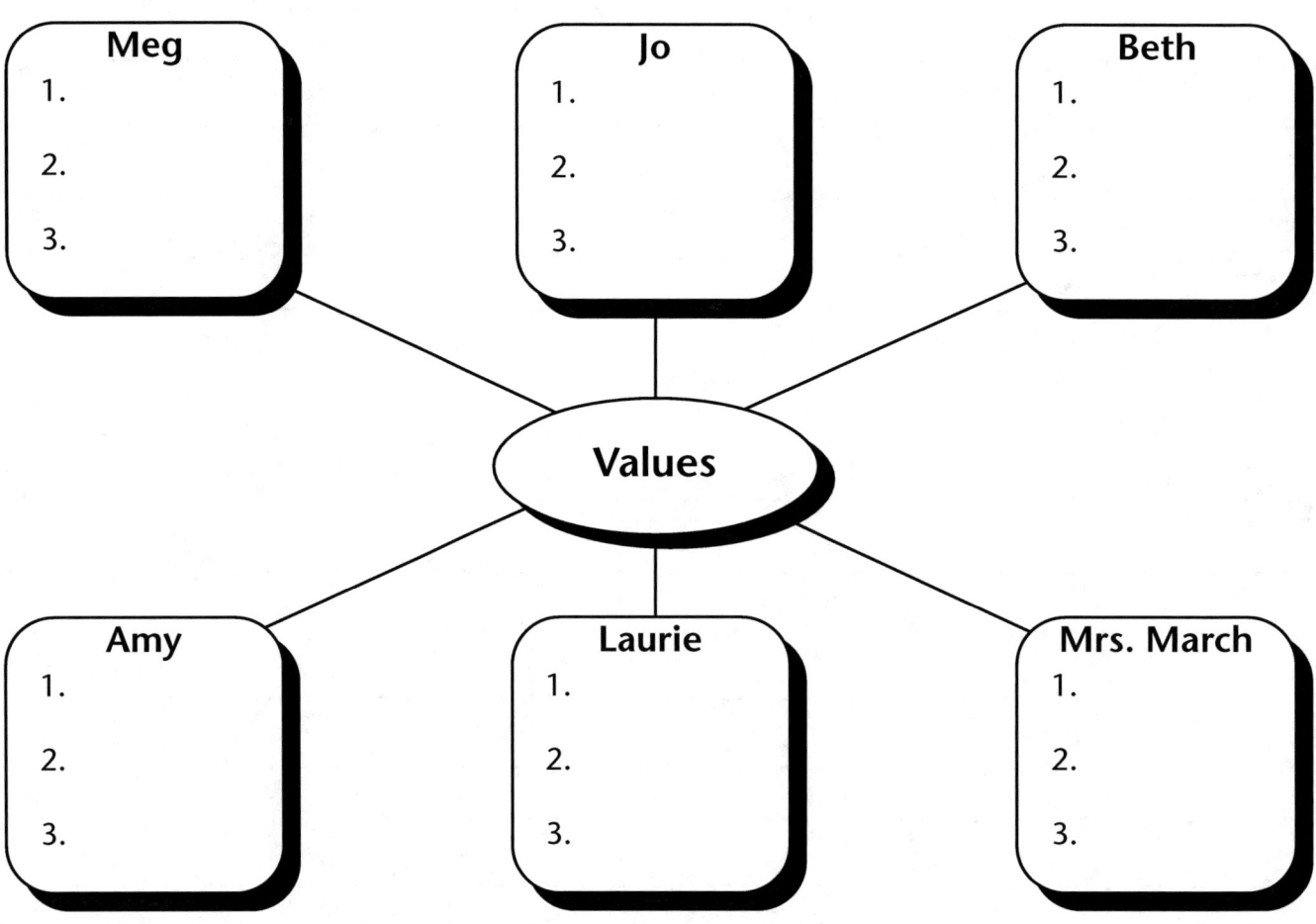

Portrait of a Character

Directions: Pick your favorite character from the story. Create a portrait collage based on your knowledge of that character. Draw the outline of a body then fill the body with pictures related to the character. Put pictures in the appropriate region of the body. *For example: You could cover Amy's hands with art supplies since she had a passion for art.* Write a brief explanation for each picture you include.

Song Lyrics

Directions: Use information from the story to create a song that represents and retells the story of the March family. Be as creative as possible.

_____

_____

_____

_____

_____

_____

_____

_____

_____

_____

_____

_____

_____

_____

_____

_____

_____

_____

Diary Entry

Directions: Pick the character to whom you best relate. Write diary entries from that character's perspective. Be sure to include all the major events in the story. Try to take on the personality of the character as much as possible.

_____

_____

_____

_____

_____

_____

_____

_____

_____

_____

_____

_____

_____

_____

_____

_____

_____

_____

Board Game

The characters in *Little Women* face many challenges on a daily basis. There were many things encountered: illness, death, war, lack of money, etc. They basically had to play "the game" to survive everyday.

Directions: Based on the novel, create your own board game that retells either the whole story or part of the story. Try to make it as creative as possible. Be sure to include the following: directions and rules, playing pieces, a board (can be posterboard), a box to contain the whole game, and any other supplies necessary to play the game. Decorate the box—it should look as if it just came off the store shelf. Make sure you have played through your game in order to get all the "kinks" out.

Once everyone has completed their games, you can have a "game day" in class. Everyone can play the various games and provide input about each one.

Directions: Read each of the following statements. Mark each statement as "True" or "False." If the answer is false, correct it so is becomes true.

_____ 1. The girls decide to give their Christmas breakfast to a needy neighbor.

_____ 2. Laurie's parents did not want to raise him so they left him with his grandfather.

_____ 3. Mr. Laurence gives Beth a piano to play.

_____ 4. Amy burns Jo's diary in order to get even with her.

_____ 5. The girls decide they enjoy life much better when they do not do any work.

_____ 6. Beth is exposed to scarlet fever while she is trying to help the Hummels.

_____ 7. Mrs. March leaves her children alone while she and Father go on vacation.

_____ 8. We are told that Mr. Brooke cares a great deal for Meg.

_____ 9. Aunt March thinks John is after Meg's money.

_____ 10. Jo is sent to live with Aunt March.

_____ 11. Aunt March tells Meg that she will never help her if she marries John.

_____ 12. Jo is happy that Meg is planning to marry John.

_____ 13. Jo is beginning to sell some of her stories to the local paper.

_____ 14. The Hummels' baby dies because the mother neglected it.

_____ 15. Jo is afraid Beth is in love with Laurie.

Name_____

Directions: Read the following questions. Write a brief (one- to two-sentence) answer for each question.

1. How is it that Laurie's money always seems to disappear?

2. According to Meg, what is the most important element needed at her wedding?

3. How does Amy think Jo acted while they were out visiting?

4. How does Jo feel about pretending to have money?

5. Why is Amy asked to go abroad instead of Jo?

6. How does Laurie's behavior change while he is away at college?

7. Why does Jo want to go away for the winter?

8. Why is it that Beth has been so upset?

9. What do Amy and Laurie discover about each other when he comes to comfort her?

10. Why does Jo go downtown during the rainstorm?

11. Why did the professor come looking for Jo?

12. What does Jo inherit?

13. What do Jo and the professor intend to do with the large house?

14. How does Jo describe the life she once wanted?

15. Who do the girls think is responsible for their happy lives?

Name_____

Multiple Choice

Directions: Read each question. Pick the correct answer.

_____ 1. Christmas will not be the same because
   A. Mother is gone
   B. there are no presents
   C. Beth is sick
   D. they have no money

_____ 2. Father has gone to war
   A. to fight
   B. as a chaplain
   C. to get away from his family
   D. none of the above

_____ 3. Jo thinks Laurie should be the happiest boy in the world because
   A. he doesn't have to deal with his parents
   B. he doesn't have to go to school
   C. his grandfather allows him to do whatever he wants
   D. he lives in a house full of books and splendor

_____ 4. Beth reminds Mr. Laurence of
   A. his granddaughter
   B. his daughter
   C. his daughter-in-law
   D. his wife

_____ 5. What does Laurie tell Meg about the way she looks at the party?
   A. He loves it.
   B. She should always dress in such a manner.
   C. He doesn't like it at all.
   D. None of the above.

_____ 6. Why does the canary die?
   A. It is old.
   B. The cat ate it.
   C. The girls did not want it anymore.
   D. No one took care of it.

_____ 7. What secret does Jo find out about?
   A. Beth loves Laurie.
   B. John loves Meg.
   C. Laurie loves Beth.
   D. Meg loves John.

_____ 8. Jo runs into Laurie late at night while she is
   A. trying to sell one of her stories
   B. working her second job
   C. going to the store for a loaf of bread
   D. none of the above

_____ 9. While Amy is at Aunt March's, she creates
   A. many stories
   B. a painting room
   C. a sanctuary
   D. none of the above

_____ 10. Mother and Father agree that Meg must be how old to get married?
   A. 18
   B. 19
   C. 20
   D. 21

_____ 11. What does Father say happened to Jo while he was away?
   A. She became more feminine.
   B. She stopped writing.
   C. She discovered that she didn't like to do hard work.
   D. She grew responsible.

_____ 12. What does Meg eventually tell John?
   A. She cannot marry him.
   B. She will marry him.
   C. She never wishes to marry.
   D. She will only marry him if the ceremony is soon.

_____ 13. When Amy planned to have a party, how many of her friends showed up on the second day?
   A. none
   B. one
   C. two
   D. three

_____ 14. What did John surprise Meg with on "jelly day"?
   A. a dinner guest
   B. flowers
   C. an invitation to go out to dinner
   D. none of the above

_____ 15. What does Jo believe to be wrong with Beth?
   A. She is dying.
   B. She is in love with John.
   C. She is in love with Laurie.
   D. She wants to go to Rome with Amy.

_____ 16. Jo tells Laurie that he flirts
   A. too much
   B. not enough
   C. too obviously
   D. incorrectly

_____ 17. How did Jo feel about the stories she had published in *The Weekly Volcano*?
   A. proud
   B. ashamed
   C. successful
   D. rich

_____ 18. When Jo leaves the professor, she tells him that she wishes to
   A. keep their friendship
   B. marry him
   C. never see him again
   D. come back and visit

_____ 19. Beth tells Jo that she believes she is
   A. in love with Laurie
   B. in need of a long vacation
   C. dying
   D. never going to marry

_____ 20. What comment did Beth make about her needle?
   A. It is too small.
   B. It is not the correct one.
   C. It is too big.
   D. It is too heavy.

_____ 21. The family received word that
   A. Amy and Laurie were going to be married
   B. Amy and Laurie were not coming home
   C. Amy and Laurie could never locate each other while they were abroad
   D. none of the above

_____ 22. Why does the wedding take place in Paris?
   A. Out of respect for Beth.
   B. It was a private ceremony.
   C. No one was invited.
   D. So the couple could travel together.

_____ 23. Who does Jo fall in love with?
   A. Laurie
   B. Mr. Laurence
   C. John
   D. Professor Bhaer

_____ 24. Amy and Laurie name their daughter after
   A. Jo
   B. Amy
   C. Beth
   D. Meg

_____ 25. All the women are
      A. happy with their lives
      B. unhappy in their marriages
      C. living at home with Mrs. March
      D. none of the above

Analysis

A. Think about the event you think is most the important in the story. How does the event change the major characters? Why do you think it is the most important event? How would the story be different without that event? Be sure you use evidence from the novel to support your ideas.

B. All the members of the March family seem to be quite content with their lives, even though they do not seem to have as much as others. What do you think is the reason for their happiness? What makes them look so favorably at each day of their lives? How could you use their knowledge to help you in your life?

Answer Key

Activities #1 and #2: Answers will vary.

Study Questions
Chapters 1-4: 1. no presents 2. at war 3. buy Mother presents 4. chaplain 5. guidebook
6. helping someone in need 7. give it to the needy family 8. angels 9. German 10. put on plays
11. Mr. Laurence—he was pleased by their good deed. 12. She was worried Father wasn't having a
good Christmas. 13. a New Year's Eve dance 14. her dress was burnt and torn on the back
15. the Laurence boy 16. sprained her ankle 17. see Mother wave 18. adopt one of the girls
19. They wanted their family to stay together. 20. her library 21. his four sons

Chapters 5-8: 1. make friends with him 2. cats and food 3. love for books 4. he's surrounded by so
many books 5. He was a fine man—brave and honest. Mr. Laurence was honored to be his friend.
6. seemed lively and vivacious 7. They died. 8. piano 9. They kept the servants away and provided her
with new music books. 10. made him slippers 11. sent Beth a piano 12. his granddaughter 13. gives
him a hug and a kiss 14. to buy pickled limes 15. told that Amy had limes 16. throw them out the
window 17. She quits and promises to study at home with Beth. 18. the theater with Laurie 19. what
Amy is going to do to make her sorry 20. her book of stories 21. burns Jo's book 22. skating with
Laurie 23. it is soft in the middle 24. Jo's isn't as bad as hers once was

Chapters 9-12: 1. with Annie Moffat 2. flowers 3. her and her mother 4. he doesn't know her and is
afraid of her 5. She says she is not Meg tonight. 6. never repeat foolish gossip and forget it as fast as
you can 7. Pickwick Club based on Dickens' characters 8. Laurie 9. a post office in the hedges 10. It is
as bad as all work and no play. 11. He died; no one took care of it. 12. salt and spoiled cream 13. a
letter encouraging and commending her efforts to control her temper 14. row to Long Meadow for
lunch and croquet 15. put a clothespin on her nose to lift it 16. Meg 17. Jo 18. go to college

Chapters 13-16: 1. in the saloon 2. She hopes he never goes in such places. 3. trying to get her stories
published 4. He knows where Meg's missing glove is 5. She is awaiting news from the paper. 6. word
that her husband is ill 7. take care of him 8. He shouldn't have joined the Army and that no good will
come of it. 9. sold her hair 10. over her hair 11. hope and keep busy 12. waving in Mother's place 13.
He is doing much better. 14. Mother's closet 15. The baby died in her arms of scarlet fever.
16. Rudely—she did not call the doctor soon enough. 17. so she will not catch the fever
18. telegraphed for Mother the day before Jo did 19. Her fever broke. 20. work 21. go through
closets and trunks 22. a place for her to worship and pray 23. create her will

Chapters 17-20: 1. She liked the idea. 2. Mary and Jesus 3. a turquoise ring 4. She will use it to remind
herself not to be selfish. 5. that Mr. Brooke fancies Meg and he kept her lost glove 6. She is too young,
and he is too poor. 7. She is aware of John's fondness for Meg, but he will not ask to marry her until he
has established a comfortable home. 8. twenty 9. She doesn't want to tell Meg the secret of John's
love. 10. She doesn't want to tell Laurie the secret. 11. Jo and Laurie 12. John cares for Meg and wishes
to know his fate before he returns. 13. responds to it 14. She is too young. 15. He said he never wrote
such a note and that Jo shouldn't be speaking of them in such a manner. 16. Laurie 17. He never
told—and never will tell—John of the notes. 18. He brings Mr. March home. 19. It is burnt, but it is far
more beautiful. 20. She has become gentler and more feminine. 21. She is not as shy. 22. learned to
think more of others than herself and has decided to carefully mold her character. 23. She has feelings

---

for him, and she now blushes. 24. He wishes to know if she cares for him. 25. She forgets it. 26. She needn't be bothered with such things. 27. She won't receive any help from her. 28. Love in a cottage can't be worse than the love some find in a big house. 29. He likes her for the money she will inherit. 30. She does care for him. 31. John sitting with Meg on his knee. 32. Sister Jo 33. his plans to take care of Meg

Chapters 21-25: 1. three years 2. He is a minister. 3. served his country but was sent home after being wounded 4. worked as a bookkeeper to establish a home for Meg 5. Meg is learning to be a wife. Amy is working for Aunt March. Jo is devoted to literature and Beth. Beth is still delicate from the fever. 6. attending college 7. her promise to never support Meg if she and John married 8. sent linens secretly 9. a watchman's rattle 10. money 11. She will be married next. 12. No one will want her. 13. people whom she loves around her 14. The informality of it all—the bride is running about and the groom is working. 15. Mr. Laurence 16. hopped away and danced with the others 17. money, positions, fashionable accomplishments, and elegant manners 18. a party for her classmates 19. it rained 20. to buy a lobster 21. She was paid $100 for a story. 22. be a model housewife and make jars of jelly 23. to never annoy anyone with their private worries and quarrels 24. bring home a friend 25. He allowed him to stay, and they had a good time by themselves. 26. Throw out the jelly and hide the pots. 27. twins 28. Mother, Grandmother, Mr. Laurence and John

Chapters 26-28: 1. social calls (visits) 2. She replied with only "yes" or "no." 3. talks to everyone and is the center of attention 4. She called her ordinary. 5. People are aware that they are poor, so why should they pretend to be otherwise? 6. as herself—enjoys being with the children 7. She chooses to be nice to the poor boy and not the rich one. 8. May was jealous of Amy. 9. To go to another table 10. flowers from Mr. Laurence's garden and boys to buy them 11. She is going abroad and wishes to take Amy with her. 12. She hated favors and French. 13. whether she has any genius 14. Laurie will go to comfort Amy, and it is quite possible that it will happen. 15. Beth's spirits 16. She is in love with Laurie. 17. He became serious and studious. 18. He flirts too much. 19. devote himself to one modest girl but finish college first 20. go away for a change and to learn something new

Chapters 29-31: 1. Professor Bhaer 2. his washing and mending 3. teach her German 4. a book of Shakespeare's work 5. Take it to the paper to have it published. 6. People want to be amused not preached at—morals don't sell nowadays. 7. Take Beth to the mountains. 8. searched newspapers, went to the library, studied faces 9. tragic—poisonings, accidents, deaths, crimes, etc. 10. his good will 11. character 12. ashamed and glad her name is not on them 13. burns them 14. keep it for a lifetime 15. pledge his love to her 16. to please Jo 17. It is impossible for people to make themselves love other people if they don't. 18. not well—He still insists on loving Jo. 19. the truth about her rejecting Laurie 20. go abroad

Chapters 32-36: 1. Grateful—she begged not to go so far. 2. no 3. She will die. 4. prepare Mother and Father and stay by their sides 5. Amy 6. handsome, tired, spiritless, older, and grave 7. She intends to court him. 8. a look of relief 9. She is a charming woman. 10. when he will return 11. She works diligently, and he chooses not to work. 12. bitter, full of pain and regret 13. if she will marry him if asked 14. With every chance to be good, useful and happy, he is faulty, lazy and miserable. 15. "So Do I!" 16. She doesn't want the people at home to be as disappointed in him as she is. 17. He is going to be with his grandfather, and she should pursue Fred. 18. They set up a room full of all the things she loves. 19. It is heavy. 20. Beth says she is stronger with Jo around. 21. She dies. 22. by showing her that a girl's rejection did not spoil his life 23. She wouldn't let him come home and said she couldn't be happy with him. 24. She told him "no." 25. by letter 26. She is told to stay and let absence soften her sorrow. 27. They are suited for each other.

Chapters 37-41: 1. ceaseless longing for Beth 2. write again 3. They are engaged. 4. well 5. twenty-five 6. They got married. 7. Aunt Carrol wouldn't let them travel together otherwise. 8. He shall never stop loving her—but it's an altered love. Amy and Jo have switched places in his heart. 9. Professor Bhaer 10. go into business and prove to Grandpa that he isn't spoiled 11. astonish them with the elegance of their mansion 12. to ask Jo to marry him 13. He wishes he were younger and richer. 14. if they love each other, it doesn't matter 15. She is happy, sings and worries about her appearance. 16. She's afraid of being laughed at after her declarations of independence. 17. to the places where men gather 18. Professor Bhaer 19. to carry her bundles 20. He will only visit once more. 21. disappointed 22. to teach at a college and provide for his boys 23. the West 24. find a dress for Tina 25. She tells him it is because he is going away. 26. could she care for him as more than a friend 27. a poem she had written 28. wait for him while he goes off to work 29. Aunt March leaves her a large home. 30. make it a school for boys 31. the yearly apple picking 32. sixty 33. Beth 34. lonely and selfish 35. happy 36. Mother

Activities #3-#25: Answers will vary. Accept reasonable answers.

Comprehension Quiz 1: 1. True 2. False (died) 3. True 4. True 5. False (they must work and play to be happy) 6. True 7. False (to take care of Father) 8. True 9. True 10. False (Amy) 11. True 12. False (not happy) 13. True 14. False (scarlet fever) 15. True

Comprehension Quiz 2: 1. He lends it to people. 2. She wanted to be surrounded by those she loved. 3. disrespectful and inappropriate 4. everyone knows they aren't rich, so why pretend 5. Jo said she hated French and favors. 6. He becomes serious and studious. 7. to allow Laurie to fall in love with Beth 8. She knows she is dying. 9. love each other 10. find the professor 11. a poem he read in the paper 12. Aunt March's house 13. boys' home 14. lonely and selfish 15. Mother

Novel Test—
Multiple Choice: 1. B 2. B 3. D 4. A 5. C 6. D 7. B 8. A 9. C 10. C 11. A 12. B 13. B 14. A 15. C 16. A 17. B 18. A 19. C 20. D 21. A 22. D 23. D 24. C 25. A
Analysis: Accept reasonable answers.